8

ESSENTIALS
TO A RACE
CONVERSATION

&
Manual to a New Dialogue

MILAGROS PHILLIPS

8 ESSENTIALS TO A RACE CONVERSATION:

A Manual to a New Dialogue

© Copyright 2016 Milagros Phillips

info@milagrosphillips.com

www.MilagrosPhillips.com

Cover Design by Milagros a. Phillips

Cover Painting: AND THEN THERE'S SUNLIGHT

Milagros A. Phillips

2016 Acrylic on Canvas 30X30

Web Art Galleries:

http://milagros-phillips.pixels.com/

TABLE OF CONTENTS

DEDICATION

I lovingly dedicate this book to my children, for whom I want a better world, to my parents, who made me believe a better world was possible, and to the ancestors who endured to make a better world possible for me.

ACKNOWLEDGEMENTS

I wish to thank the following people for their help in creating this book and for their contributions to my inspiration: My courageous ancestors; my children who lovingly encourage me to create; Cheryl Jamison, Dawn Longenecker, Ginny Baldwin, and Lisa Peters, for sharing their experiences. My friends Susan Hadler, Ginny Baldwin, and Kathy Gille, for encouragement feedback, and great questions; Deirdre Mcglynn for her constant support of my work; and my editor Leslie Lass.

INTRODUCTION

Race is America's conversation taboo. We talk a lot about it, protest about it, scream and yell about it, hide in shame about it, and make jokes about it, but how often do we stop to have a real conversation about race?

Conversations require civility. They require quiet listening, time, and energy. They also require care—care for self and care for others who are part of the interchange. Conversations are an exchange of ideas and a sharing of experiences that, when done well, leave us better off than we were when we started. Conversations, in short, can change lives.

Whether the conversation is one on one, you lead or are part of a group. Conversations on race are essential to the health of America. These conversations are vital to the wellbeing of our organizations, institution, and communities.

For conversations on race to change lives, though, they need to be handled with sensitivity, with an awareness of the topic through race literacy and with a desire to allow these experiences to touch the heart. Too often we want to talk about the research on race and want to turn the conversation on race into an academic exercise; yet, while research is necessary and while the academics give us the historical background we need to allow the emotions. The real work on race is the work of the heart. If problems related to race were just cognitive ones, we would have solved them a long time ago, but issues about race are emotional, and if we are ever going to change people's hearts we need to appeal to their emotions.

Race needs to be part of the conversation in every facet of American life. Before any major decision is made at federal and state levels, for instance, race needs to be considered because it impacts housing, education, healthcare, and politics. It determines something as mundane as, how many supermarkets (versus fast food places) will be in a particular neighborhood, how many green spaces and parks will be available in a given location, and how many clinics and hospitals will be built.

Race affects how the nation's resources will be distributed, how, where, and whether money will be invested in communities. What philanthropists will and will not contribute to. What children will receive on their lunch trays at school, and so much more. The ways that race impacts American lives could fill volumes, so learning to bring race into important conversations is a necessary skill to have, if we are to change the impact of race on our daily lives.

A courageous conversation

On February 18, 2009, during a Black History Month speech given to Department of Justice employees, America's first black Attorney General, Eric Holder, accused Americans of being cowards when it came to having a conversation on race.

"Though this nation has proudly thought of itself as an ethnic melting pot," he said, *"in things racial we have always been and continue to be, in too many ways, essentially a nation of cowards."*

He went on to say that Americans are afraid to talk about race, adding that, *"certain subjects are off-limits and that to explore them risks, at best embarrassment, and, at worst, the questioning of one's character."*

In his speech, Holder challenged America to use Black History Month not only to celebrate African American history but also *"to foster a dialogue between the races."* I took what he said to heart.

After all, I had been having conversations on race for more than 20 years, and, though some had been rather challenging, most had been largely successful.

For about 15 years I had been leading small- and large-group seminars on healing racism and had managed to change many hearts. So, after hearing Attorney General Holder speak, I decided to do what I love to do—engage perfect strangers in a conversation on race. I simply wanted to see what would happen.

To begin, I should say that, when I engage in a conversation on race, it is not to convince anyone of anything; it is simply to share with others what I have experienced, what I have learned from these experiences, and what I have come to believe and know. It is up to the individual to change his or her mind.

I trust people to make good decisions about their own inner development, but I know that, in order for them to do so, they need good information. So, for three days I sat at a DuPont Circle Starbucks, in February of 2009 in Washington, DC, with a tent sign that read, "Join me in a COURAGEOUS CONVERSATION on RACE." As people passed by my table I would look them in the eyes, hoping to ignite their interest. Some would put their heads down and continue walking, and some would look back at me and smile, but even the ones who smiled did not seem interested enough to engage with me.

After a few hours, a young white man, who seemed to be in his late twenties, joined me. He was from the Midwest, he told me, and was on vacation. I asked him if he had heard the Attorney General's speech, and he said he had. He also said that he thought the nation had come a long way and that our election of a black president proved as much. This was not a surprising comment at the time.

After the election of our 44th president, Barak Obama, many people felt that we were living in a "post-racial society."

For them, this meant that we no longer had to talk about or deal with race in any way, and it also meant that a conversation on race was not only taboo, but was passé, and out of sync with the progress we had clearly made.

I asked him how much he knew about African American history, and he said he did not know much. I asked him about his knowledge of Native American history, or about the history of Chinese Americans and Japanese Americans, and he said he had seen some documentaries about the First and Second World Wars. I then asked him if he knew about the internment camps that held people of Japanese descent during the Second World War, and he said he had never heard of these camps but promised to look up information about them on the Internet when he had a chance.

Since I wasn't getting much attention, after meeting with this young man I decided to try and engage the people already seated with their coffee and tea, but as I approached them they looked at me as if I were a homeless person asking for money. After several hours of this, an African American woman finally asked me what I was doing.

I invited her to sit with me and told her I was a diversity consultant who specialized in issues related to race. I also told her I had heard the Attorney General's speech and had taken to heart his call for us to engage each other in courageous conversations on the topic. She thought it was a great idea and wished me luck, with a sad smile, and a sigh.

She told me she had heard the speech, so I asked her what she had thought of it. She said she agreed with the Attorney General. "Race," she said, "is one of those things that is hard to talk about." She then told me that, at her job, she had had several unpleasant racial encounters with some of her white co-workers and had a hard time bringing up the matter to her boss for fear that he would be dismissive or would accuse her of being overly sensitive. She was also concerned that he would treat her with suspicion if she reported the racial incidents or that revelations about her colleagues would strain her work relationship. She also feared that speaking out would put her job at risk. She ended our conversation by saying she was grateful for what I was doing but that she thought my efforts would probably not make much of a difference. Yet, the desire to make a difference is the driving force that leads us to do something, even when our efforts are not seen as successful.

In 2015, in the midst of national protest over police killing black men, the CEO of Starbucks, Howard Schultz, wanted to do something about race discourse and used Starbucks to try and make a difference. It made sense; Americans love their coffee, and his company had access to untold numbers of people on a daily basis.

In the hopes of sparking a dialogue about racial inequality, the baristas (those who prepare and serve the coffee) at Starbucks were instructed to write on the customers' cups the words *"Race Together as a way to spark a conversation on race,"* but instead the campaign inspired criticism.

In his March 2015 article "Starbucks Baristas Will Stop Writing 'Race Together' on Your Cups," former *Time* reporter Jack Linshi wrote, *"The initiative has attracted controversy as a well-intentioned yet ineffective method to generate more conversations about the topic in a bid to influence change in the wake of racially charged events, like the nationwide protests over police brutality and several officer-involved killings of unarmed black Americans."*

The attempt was a stark reminder of how these conversations need to be initiated with more than just a spark of good intentions. This short book is borne out of the conviction that courageous conversations on race are both necessary and possible. I offer some guideposts out of my own years of experience facilitating many such conversations.

But race conversations are difficult even for those who have been trained to facilitate them. The reality is that people often come to these conversations angry, wounded, or with unrealistic expectations. Managing emotions becomes the most important task of a facilitator, and that's not always easy.

Although this book is about having a conversation on race, the process is universal and the book is written for both participant and facilitator. Conversations, challenging or peasant, can benefit from the process outlined in this book. I wrote this book because in 25 years of doing this work I have seen people change more than their minds; I have seen them change their hearts. I wrote about some of them in my first book, *11 REASONS TO BECOME RACE LITERATE: A pocket guide to a new conversation*. One senior VP of a Fortune 100 company said, *"I have attended a lot of seminars in my professional career, but none have impacted me the way that seminar on race touched me. I thought I was doing all the right things. I didn't know that I was doing them from my own racial conditioning and that has made all the difference to me."* My experiences have shown me that change is possible.

SELF-PREPARATION

Self-preparation, awareness, and compassion for self and others, are the most valuable tools we bring to any conversation about race. Race-related research about past or current state of the country, done by a reputable institution, such as a university and some knowledge of African American history (beyond what was taught in school) are added gifts that expand the conversation and that allow for greater learning.

In leading or participating in a conversation on race, take a few moments to breathe with all of those who are present. The breath unites us in ways that are immeasurable. Allow a sense of calm to be present in you as the facilitator, or participant. Experience the peace in your own breath, and gently break the silence to start introductions. Allow all participants the opportunity to say their names and to share whatever is in their hearts.

Set an intention for the conversation. Is the conversation to look at the impact of race on organizational policy? Is it for neighbors to know each other better? Is it to speak about an issue in the community? Is it a follow-up to a race incident? Whatever the intention, you have come together primarily to speak about the issue of race, so be clear about that from the start. There is already enough confusion out there about this topic, and you don't want to add to it. Rather, set an intention that this conversation will add to clarity, community, and collective oneness.

Be prepared for the healing crisis, resistance, and hijackers. Even when people come to the race conversation willingly, they are still carrying their own issues with the topic and something shared can become a trigger. A trigger is something that when you hear it throws you emotionally off kilter.

Don't let that put you off, though. People get triggered because they are carrying unprocessed internal pain, which manifests as ammunition that can explode when triggered. Do your best to remain internally quiet, and compassionately understanding even when individuals in the group express pain and anger. Remember, also, that these kind and caring responses can be disarming.

As you begin your conversation on race, create a space of peace within yourself, and make room for miracles. These conversations, while challenging, can be magical. When you work on yourself first you learn your gifts and your limitations. You learn to clear your own inner pain and fill your own heart with peace and compassion. You begin to see your own ignorance, denial, and anger, and you begin to heal. That healing allows you to become the light that lets all other lights shine. By sharing your story you give permission to all other members of your group to tell their story, creating a bond of safety that nurtures all those who are involved in the conversation.

Having an experience of safety is very important to the conversation. Here is what one former participant, a writer and now a friend, had to say about her experience:

"I met Milagros Philips about 14 years ago when she arrived in Battle Creek, Michigan, as the first Executive Director of The National Resource Center for the Healing of Racism. The year before, she had been invited by the Kellogg Foundation as an expert-in-residence to give talks and hold town hall meetings on racial healing. The foundation was very impressed, as were the attendees, and she immediately won the hearts of those who heard her.

I took the first seminar she offered, which was made up of black and white members who had come out of hope and curiosity, but there was discomfort and we self-segregated in our choice of chairs. Milagros promised a non-threatening environment, which was hard to believe given our racial history.

Then Milagros performed the miracle, which I saw continue through four of her seminars that I attended. And it was talked about among the participants. These seminars were not only intelligent and informative; they were non-threatening, as she promised. Bonds and understanding developed between blacks and whites. Pain was explored, yet all were protected by her goodness and spiritual grace. While the participants discussed painful racial experiences, Milagros transcended effortlessly to represent a time and space where only individual souls mattered and race faded. It was a moving journey considering the pain involved, but everyone on the journey learned from this woman, who led us to the door of racial history and experience yet was beyond race herself. We followed her example unconsciously and were absorbed into this loving *and non-threatening environment, which transcended the very sorrows that brought us together and made us all, better than we were at the beginning."*

What Ginny didn't know at the time was the deep preparation I underwent in order to do my seminar from a place of inner peace. I had to learn to manage my triggers and to be conscious of my own emotions, to get to a place where I could do this work with some sense of inner peace. I knew as the convener that I had responsibility for what I brought into that space. I had to work through a lot of anger. In the mid-eighties I embarked on a journey of inner healing, balance, and transformation. I knew that there was something wrong, but could not quite put my finger on what it was. I had done all that I was supposed to do, get an education, get married, have and care for a family, be successful at doing my work. Yet, my jobs didn't pay me the same wages as my white office mates. When I graduated college, my white friends were all getting hired in our field (the fashion industry), but I couldn't find a job. I had to go into sales to support myself, a field that I eventually came to appreciate. I eventually got a job as an assistant manager at E.J. Korvettes, a department store in New York. One of my jobs was to train the new recruits. I was twenty-four at the time, hardworking and ambitious. I was married with a three-year-old and a five-month-old. I had trained three white young men, who had gone into the management program. I asked my boss when I would be going into the program. It was one of the reasons I had taken the job. He simply said, "you're not ready." I was really angry. All I knew was that I was good enough to train, but not good enough to go into the management training program to advance my career. I was in pain. I felt cheated, violated and angry. I remember wondering if there was something wrong with me?

A few years later I had gone back to school for a degree in business and I had to write a thesis. Since

I was already doing some work in diversity, I decided to write my theses on race. I read everything I could get my hands on that was race related, but mostly I read about healing. As I delved deeper into the research and I began to learn the history of race in America, a history I had not learned in school. I began to understand racism and to uncover its many faces. As I went deeper into my healing, I encountered an anger that seemed like an abyss. I thought I would never stop being angry.

I remember spending a weekend in silence, as one of my meditation practices, and uncovering a rage that I didn't know existed in me. Unwilling to break my commitment to my silence, I had no choice but to allow the rage and to accept it. I had to be silent with it and at times I felt as if I would explode. My heart was beating so hard I could hear it in my ears. My whole body was vibrating with anger. After what seemed like forever, the feeling began to fade, and a feeling of peace came over me. What became available to me on that day has stayed with me. I learned that peace was a constant and that I had the power to choose it.

That day I allowed peace to choose me. In spite of this I still had grief to work through, and that in and of itself was a journey. I had to grieve the incredible losses I had experienced in my life due to my ignorance and lack of understanding of institutional racism, and how racism works.

In the early days of facilitating my seminar "Transformation Race and Healing," I remember a participant in Battle Creek, Michigan, who offered to share a video with me. On the second day of our two-day seminar, he arrived an hour early, just as I was checking the technology to make sure everything worked properly before everyone arrived. He had brought me a copy of a History Channel documentary called, "The Night Tulsa Burned," and we began to watch it together, along with a visiting colleague who was co-facilitating with me on that day.

It was about forty-five minutes long, so I figured we would be finished in time to start the morning check-in. As I watched the documentary I was mesmerized. The participants began to arrive while we were still watching the video and they were shocked by what they were seeing. None of us had ever heard of this historical event; certainly we had not read about it in history books. It was the biggest race riot in American history. The only one who knew about it was the man who had brought the tape, and, he had found out about the riot from the documentary. Prior to that, he had never heard of it either. Now the video is available all over the internet, but sixteen years ago, it was on VHS.

We watched as a white mob burned and looted the black section of Tulsa, Oklahoma, known as the Greenwood section, also known as "Black Wall-Street," where segregation had forced African

Americans to create their own thriving economy. Black Tulsa had a high level of black-owned businesses and home ownership. After the riot, white Tulsans went on as if nothing had happened, while black Tulsans were left to rebuild on their own with no city assistance. The incident was sparked by the rumor that a young white woman, who was an elevator operator in 1921, had been raped by a young black man who used the only restroom available to blacks. The restroom was on the top floor of the Drexel building, in the all-white section of Tulsa, where the black man worked as a shoe shine (shoe black). What was known about the incident was that the woman was screaming when the young man ran out of the elevator.

To make matters worse, the white Tulsans cut the article that incited the riot out of the bound copies of "The Tulsa Tribune" newspaper, blamed the riot on the black community, and enacted ordinances that made it difficult for the blacks to rebuild, while trying to steal the land from the black citizens. It is estimated that four hundred African Americans died during the riot, and the entire community was turned to rubble, its citizens left traumatized and homeless. The woman never pressed charges against the black man, and she left town, as did he when he was exonerated.

We watched the whole program, and the video became part of our morning check-in. In disbelief, one white male said angrily, *"I didn't know about this. Why didn't I know about this?"* But nothing could have prepared me for what happened next.

Luckily I had invited my friend and colleague Walter LeFlore, an African- American man from Massachusetts with a great deal of facilitation experience, to co-facilitate the seminar with me. I saw that he was visibly moved, and, as participants shared their experiences with the video, grief, sadness, and fear all welled up in me at once.

One African-American man shared his experiences and feelings related to the death of Emmet Till. He told us about being a young teen and about not feeling safe, and he said he knew that the police would not keep him safe and that not even his parents could ensure his safety. He spoke about living a life without sanctuary, and I began to cry. Even as I write this, I can still feel the sadness of it all. He said he was 67 years old and he had never in his entire life felt really safe.

I asked Walter to take over, excused myself, went to the lady's room, and began to cry uncontrollably. For some reason, something I had been carrying within me broke that day and shattered into pieces. I became aware of a feeling I had unconsciously carried with me all my life, one that had colored everything: I, myself, had never really felt safe! I had just soldiered on with my life unaware of the great courage that it took to be me! Until then I had been unaware of the great composure it took to move past the daily slights and unending insults, to tiptoe through life in fear of waking some sleeping giant.

I let myself cry, washed my face, went back into the room, and shared my realization with the group in an attempt to be present and authentic. That morning, other people shared how little they knew about African-American history and how they had never really given it much thought. They realized how important it was for their own process of growth, to gain a deeper understanding of this missing history and to see how it helped to put things in perspective.

From personal experience, I also learned the value of something I had been aware of in my seminars from the time I had started facilitating: the value of allowing emotions to surface. Emotions are an important part of the healing process and are extremely valuable to our conversations. By learning to process our emotions, we understand the power of that process and we are more likely to make room for the emotions of the participants. Clearing our emotions opens us up to become a living bridge from what was to what can be.

Prepare to be criticized

Remember the expression, "Don't shoot the messenger?" Well, prepare to be shot with criticism. While most people don't want the responsibility of leading a conversation on race, they often have very particular ideas of what the conversation should look like and how it should be led. Don't let negative comments throw you.

Be discerning about what is yours and what belongs to others. Among other criticisms, I have on occasion been accused of preaching to the choir—mostly by whites who feel that the audience should include people who are "really racist." When I first started doing race seminars I used to take what they said to heart until one day I realized that it was not my responsibility to invite the "really racist people who need to hear the message" to the conversation. My responsibility was to invite participants, make the environment safe, and facilitate the conversation.

While the comment about "singing to the choir" criticism is valid, as a black woman I am less likely to have access to people who are openly racist than are whites. Whites are more likely than I to know who in their community could benefit from a seminar on racial healing, as they are more likely to be the ones hearing the racist conversations, which people feel safe to share in their presence. They also are more likely to have the racist parents, the racist aunts and uncles, and the racist work colleague. So if they know where the choir is singing and they don't expose those who need it to the song, that's on them, not on the facilitator. So don't take it to heart.

You can prepare yourself to be an effective convener of conversations about race by doing some journaling about your experiences with race and by processing your emotions about these experiences. Learning to deal effectively with your own pain about this thing we call race makes you more effective in being with the pain that will arise in others as you enter the arena of these conversations.

Processing is very important. Do your best to build it into the conversation. "Processing" is more than just trying to make sense of information. It means taking in information and allowing it to move through our mind, body, spirit, and emotions. Processing allows for a catharsis that can come from a realization, and it allows us to see how we fit into the new information, how the new information fits in us, and how the new information makes us feel (More about processing later in the book).

To summarize, when you work on yourself first, you learn your gifts and your limitations. You become the light that allows all others to shine. By sharing your history with race, you give permission to the other members of the group to share theirs, creating a bond that nurtures all involved.

1.THE SETUP

Before beginning a conversation on race, it is imperative to realize that in our nation the daily reality of blacks and non-blacks is very different. Participants at these conversations are apt to differ in their views, opinions, and beliefs about the American experience. It is therefore vital that we listen to those with the experiences, as well as sharing our own. If you haven't lived it, you need to listen to those who have.

Where is the conversation taking place?

Is it in an organization, or an institution? Is it in a community setting, a town hall meeting, or a school? Where the conversation is taking place and the number of people attending will determine the structure of that conversation and even the placement of the chairs.

Setting the purpose

A successful race conversation offers facts for the head and experiences for the heart. Without the experiential work that touches the heart, a conversation on race becomes another academic exercise—a lot of great information but none of the experiences that lead to transformation. Prepare to show part of a documentary, or to engage the group in a meaningful exercise.

To have a successful conversation on race, all parties should come to the table with some sense of their own biases and prejudices and should be open to uncovering new ones. Conscious awareness of one's personal history with race and one's personal triggers can set the foundation for growth and understanding. It helps to decipher feelings and emotions and it gives us a foundation for why we react the way we do around the subject of race.

Knowing our background and history, including our family history with the topic, can go a long way in helping us stay present with what is happening in the conversation at any given point. We need our history for healing and transformation. Understanding who we were helps us see who we are, and it gives us the opportunity to envision who we are becoming.

The purpose

What is the purpose of the conversation? Is it to teach, to learn, to persuade, to negotiate? Is it to share, to understand, or to process emotions after a traumatic event? Is the purpose of the conversation to grieve a loss, to create an action plan, or simply to get to know one another? We need to get clear about the purpose because the purpose will drive the direction of the conversation.

The participants

Who are the participants? Will the conversation take place with a homogeneous group or with a multicultural group of people? Is the conversation a one-on-one? Is it a town hall conversation? How many people will engage in the conversation? How long do you plan to spend engaging? What do you hope to be the outcome of the conversation? How will you know if you have achieved it? If you get lost in the conversation, how will you get back on track? What will you do with the emotions that arise? Will there be a follow-up to the conversation?

The importance of time

Because conversations on race can be intense, consider facilitating a minimum of three conversations with the same group of people. This gives participants time to process their experiences from the first conversation and formulate questions they could not articulate the first time. Going away and coming back together can be very powerful. During your time away you will have time to think, to process, to explore, to research. You should, at the very least, give yourself and your colleagues the time to sleep on it.

I learned the importance of giving people time to process and began to hold two-day seminars very early on. I find that participants come back the next morning with a renewed sense of the previous day's experience. While sleeping, they process the information and are able to answer a lot of their own questions. The time away gives everyone a chance to reconcile the new information with the information they had, create inner space, and allows them to hold more information.

Follow-up

Follow-up is very important. Conversations on race create new questions about ourselves and about our lives. They awaken memories and experiences long forgotten. This is where follow-up can be helpful, especially if the original group remains intact. Having people with whom we have had a shared experience, gives us the opportunity to express without feeling judged and opens the door to exponential growth and learning. Planning for three or more conversations lets the participants know that they will not be left alone with whatever the experience awakens in them.

For years I have been doing a nine-week program that takes participants through eight stages of healing and transformation. I lead the participants on a weekly odyssey that includes observation, journaling, and research. We look at where we are in the healing continuum, and how what we are learning fits into our lives (more about the healing process in the next book). We all grow exponentially during those nine weeks. At the end of the program participants view race from an entirely different perspective as they learn to own their emotions around race and their experiences in a powerful way regardless of the color of their skin.

Setting rules of engagement

The rules of engagement are the ground rules that help us create a safe space for participants to share their experiences. They are the cornerstones of the conversation and give us a place to return to should we get lost in the process. These ground rules include rules for speaking and for listening. They are about respecting the experiences of all participants and about allowing the expression of all feelings and emotions. They also are about reminding participants that everyone is responsible for his or her feelings and emotions, which means that what you are hearing in the conversation is awakening certain feelings in you. And they are about guaranteeing the anonymity of each participant, should that be their desire.

These conversations are not places to set blame, point a finger, or accuse anyone of wrongdoing. Rather they are for informing, sharing, and expressing thoughts and feelings in an environment of compassion and care. Setting ground rules for sharing and listening can go a long way towards making the speaker feel heard and towards giving space for the listeners to process what they are hearing. Keep in mind that even with the ground rules, emotions may escalate as people express long-held views and forgotten experiences.

Here are 20 ground rules you may find helpful. The rules apply to both participants and facilitators

1. Make room for silence, even when it is uncomfortable
2. Encourage sharing, but make sure everyone knows it is voluntary
3. Let participants know that everything shared in the space stays in the space
4. Give everyone an opportunity to express his or her views
5. Respect the experience and knowledge of all participants
6. No talking while others are sharing
7. No "eye kissing" (rolling your eyes or lips from side to side or winking to signal to another participant your feelings about what is being shared)
8. No sidebar conversations
9. Listen with an open heart and an open mind
10. Make "I" statements "I think," "I feel"

11. Allow participants to emote

12. Allow yourself to feel

13. Allow for the feelings of others

14. Stay open to the process

15. Allow for change and transformation

16. No hijacking the conversation

17. Be aware of resistance from self and others

18. Avoid finger pointing

19. Avoid blaming

20. Make eye contact

You don't have to use all of these. Feel free to pick and choose the ones you feel are appropriate to your group. Always remember that racism is an inherited dysfunction. Compassion is needed for all involved.

Creating a safe space

Make the place where you are meeting as comfortable as possible. In my early days of doing this work, I always brought flowers into the space. Flowers, with their beautiful colors and fragrance, can lend an element of warmth to any space where you are holding your conversations.

Conversations are important! They are precursors to change. How we set up a conversation and how we conduct ourselves make a vast difference in our ability to impact change. It is also important to understand the intention behind our words. When a conversation necessarily elicits painful memories and painful experiences, how we broach that conversation determines how successful it will be. Race can be a "toxic" topic, as it is harsh, and can be, in many ways, harmful. It also can be an emotional topic. For a race conversation to be successful, those engaged in it must create a safe space for all the participants. The above rules can be helpful in creating that space of safety. Do your best and remember that even with your best intentions and planning, there may still be those who feel threatened and unsafe by the experience.

Your history with race

Everyone has a racial history—even the participant who says, "My first experience with someone of a different race was when I went to college." That's their history and their experience! It's not good or bad, right or wrong. It just is. Each person's history is important, and coming to the conversation with awareness of one's personal history with race can go a long way in understanding whatever reactions and feelings arise during the conversation. It can also help us keep track of our triggers, and it can help us feel where the emotions are lodged in your body (more in book three about the healing process).

Encountering differences

A study done by the Pew Research Center shows a significant difference in perceptions based on race.

"These findings are based on a national survey by Pew Research Center conducted Feb. 29-May 8,

2016, among 3,769 adults (including 1,799 whites, 1,004 blacks and 654 Hispanics).2 The survey – and the analysis of the survey findings – is centered primarily around the divide between blacks and whites and on the treatment of black people in the U.S. today."

According to the study, the percentage of those saying that blacks are treated less fairly varies widely. This research is based on non-Hispanic blacks and non-Hispanic whites.

EXPERIENCE		
	WHITES	**BLACKS**
Dealing with the police		
	50%	84%
In the courts		
	43%	75%
When applying for loan or mortgage		
	25%	66%
In the workplace		
	22%	64%
In stores and restaurants		
	21%	49%
When voting in elections		
	20%	43%

This list is just the tip of the iceberg. Be prepared to encounter all sorts of differences and to learn how even your closest friends have been affected by this thing we call race.

NOTES

2. HISTORY

Everyone and everything has a history. As each moment passes into another, that which is becomes what was, leaving us with clear and unclear memories. Regardless of how we amass that history, it is personal and it becomes part of what we carry into our conversations.

None of us was born with an actual knowledge of race as a separating factor between humans. It was something we learned from our environment and from our circle of influence, which is made up of family; community; corporate and private systems; politics; media; peers; and the placement of what we call home, be it urban, suburban, or rural. Our circle of influence helps to form our world view. And our worldview forms the filters through which we experience life.

Our history is an array of experiences colored by our emotions, whether they are positive, neutral, intense, or negative. Our history forms our character, informs our experiences, and determines how we will act in a given moment or in a particular situation. It precedes us, as our yesterdays become a protective shield that we hide behind. And, unless we have conscious awareness of that history, it can run our lives. When it comes to race, everyone has a history. Whether that history means you grew up in a homogeneous community or you were raised by liberal parents who believed that racism was wrong, you nevertheless have some connection to race in America. And this is where our conversation begins because racism is personal as much as it is collective, historical, and institutional. Our history with race matters and is an important part of what we bring to the conversation.

So, what did you learn about race? What did you learn from your parents, other adults, the media, your school, and your peers? Was race included or omitted from the conversation at home and at school? Did you receive positive or negative information about race relations? What was the racial makeup of the people in your town, your school, and your family? Who were your heroes growing up? Were there any heroes in your life who did not look like you? Who were the people featured in paintings at your museums? Did they look like you? Who were the stars in your movies? Did they look like you? Did both your parents go to college? Did they own their own home? Did you go on summer vacations, to summer camp, or to music school? Did your school get brand new books every year? Did your school have computers, a swimming pool, a ski club, and international travel? Do you remember your first experience with race? I purposely did not want to give these questions categories rather I wanted them to represent the wandering of the mind, as we begin to uncover the layers of our racial conditioning.

Answering all of these questions is important because the one person you bring to any conversation on race is you, and it's essential for you to know yourself within the context of race. What frightens you about a conversation on race? Do you feel you might be called out, called a name, be accused of something? Does the conversation bring up feelings of anger, shame, guilt, mistrust, or disconnection? Examine your feelings and be aware that you bring those feelings into the conversation as part of your personal background.

Just as human beings have a history, so, too, do events. It is helpful to understand that history. Has this event happened before? Where and to whom? Was the issue resolved? All of this information can help you come to the conversation prepared to have a more informed exchange. Those who come to the conversation may have a personal or family experience with the event in question or some other painful event, and their purpose for coming may be different than the purpose set for the conversation. Situations in which people are grieving the loss of a loved one need to be navigated with compassion and care.

Prepare for overtime

While race is not one of those conversations people typically jump to attend, when they start talking about race they find that they have a great deal to say. For some, their years of silence create a need to speak at length when they find an audience willing to listen to them, so the conversation can easily run beyond the time allotted; nevertheless, watch your time. Give everyone an opportunity to speak, and, if someone wants to continue the conversation beyond the time allocated, do your best to honor this need by offering to stay a few additional minutes, if you can. Close the conversation by letting others know that the time for this conversation is now over and those who choose to stay may do so.

3. EXPERIENCE
(Something That Touches the Heart)

I have heard it said that the heart measures time by experiences. If this is so, some of us are older than our years. In my seminars, I use film to create experiences that touch the heart of the participants. Film gives visual content that stimulates the imagination and helps illustrate another's life experience. Unless you are a person of color, you are not going to know what racial oppression feels like. But you may have an awareness of what bullying feels like, what loss and grief feel like, and what not fitting in feels like. You may also know what it feels like to not be safe, not be welcomed, or not belong. Now imagine these experiences becoming a lifestyle, where everything in life is colored by those painful events and if that were not enough, your country has institutionalized your pain.

There are countless daily slites that accrue: When you are passed over for promotion time and time again, or when you are seated at the back of a restaurant, or when a store clerk asks everyone else but you if they need help, or when a valet acts as if you are invisible and assists a customer who arrived after you did, you might begin to wonder if it was because of the color of your skin.

We all know that living in today's world can be stressful. But when you add to that the daily stress of being a person of color, particularly if you have a significant amount of melanin in your skin, you create a situation that can go as far as affecting your health. Take, for instance, what the Centers for Disease Control and Prevention (CDC) have to say about pregnancy, childbirth, and infant mortality rates (which it measures by the number of deaths per thousand births): *"There are obvious differences in infant mortality by age, race, and ethnicity; for instance, the mortality rate for non-*

Hispanic black infants is more than twice that of non-Hispanic white infants."

The CDC goes on to say that "*pregnancy-related health outcomes are influenced by factors such as race, ethnicity, age, and income, but most importantly—a woman's health.*" And, interestingly, next to this article is a purple sign that reads, "*Get healthy before you get pregnant.*" But if we are to think of health as related to the whole being, we have to consider daily stressors, physical environment, historical trauma, economic positioning, and countless other nuances that make up the experiences of an individual.

In *Unnatural Causes: Is Inequality Making Us Sick*, the creators of a documentary produced by California News Reel say "*It turns out there's much more to our health than bad habits, healthcare or unlucky genes. The social condition in which we are born, live and work profoundly affect our well-being and longevity.*"

In "When the Bough Breaks," a 28-minute segment of the four-hour documentary that focuses on infant mortality rates as well as on preterm (under 37 weeks) and low birth-weight babies, we also learn that *"researchers are circling in on the added burden of racism through the life course as a long-term risk factor."*

The research further shows that *"African-American women with graduate degrees still face a greater risk of delivering pre-term, low birth-weight babies than white women who didn't finish high school."*

Again the CDC, referring to infant mortality rates, says, *"This rate is often used as an indicator to measure the health and well-being of a nation."* Consider this while America boasts being one of, if not the richest country in the world, we have the fifth highest infant mortality rate in the world, 6.5 deaths per thousand live births according to the World Health Organization. Turkey has the highest at 13.5 deaths per thousand, and Luxenberg the lowest at 1.9 deaths per thousand.

Beyond diet and exercise, life-course stress has been found to be a significant factor affecting heart disease, diabetes, obesity, and ultimately longevity.

When we come together to speak about our experiences with race, we need to remember that while we live in a country of "equality" our experiences are far from equal. At the same time, it takes great courage and strength to live and thrive under systems of oppression, in particular racial oppression, whether we are conscious of it or not. The extra effort that racism extracts from people of color takes its toll on the health and wellbeing of the community. We see it in higher incidents of high blood pressure, diabetes, and countless other illnesses. From birth to death, people of color face greater odds and stressors that are spared from the lives of their white counterparts. But whites are not completely spared from the experiences of racism.

For some whites, the awareness of having the odds fixed in their favor, without their consent or request, brings up feelings of culpability, shame and fear. Whites carry an internalized fear of the revolt that is rarely ever discussed. This unconscious and mostly unmentioned fear has led to the over-policing of non-white populations.

Coming to a conversation about a topic that brings up these feelings isn't easy. Finding out that things are not as equal as you might have thought is jarring to the belief system and can throw one into cognitive dissonance. That's not comfortable! Yet, we all need to join the conversation to find out what we don't know and to work together to transform the situation.

As you encounter difficult moments in the conversation, remember to BREATHE. Breath is flowing life, and when you breathe you bring the flow of life into those places within you that were lifeless or stuck. Breathe slowly and deliberately. Breathe into the parts of your body where you feel the discomfort.

More often than not, it's not the conversation that made you feel uncomfortable. If you are experiencing discomfort, the discomfort was already there. All the conversation did was to bring it to the surface. The good news is that you can now clear it by accepting how you feel in the moment and by using the breath to move the energy of the discomfort. It takes a lot of energy to hold discomfort in place, especially if it was so deep inside of you that you didn't realize it was there. When you clear it, you suddenly have energy to do other things in your life.

An important note

African Americans, have only really experienced some sense of freedom since the Civil Rights Movement – a mere fifty years ago. If you stop to examine the strides that African Americans have made in this relatively short period of time, is staggering! African American men and women are involved in science and technology (from Astronauts to inventors), in education (all phases, including large numbers of Ph.D.), in media, sports, the arts (visual and performed), in medicine. Now consider the odds against them, the daily stressors, and the institutional racism, the accomplishments are nothing short of amazing.

Can you imagine what this country would be like if all people had equal rights? Who would be as a nation if we mined the wealth within every individual, by allowing them access to an excellent education and job opportunity. Can you imagine how wealthy a nation we would be if no child had to be raised in poverty, because their two and three job-holding parents, were actually paid a living wage? The possibilities are mind boggling!

4. THE CONVERSATION

"The facts ma'am; just the facts." (Joe Friday, *Dragnet*)

Telling

Our stories are an important part of us. They capture the essence of our experiences. Sometimes, though, they get muddled with our emotions, and it becomes hard to decipher between fact and fiction. They become a mixture of what actually happened, how we felt at the moment, and what meaning we attached to events. For instance, imagine you are a little child in school. The teacher asks you a question that you are not able to answer. Perhaps this is how you have processed the experience: 1) Fact: The teacher asked you a question and you did not have the answer. 2) Feeling: You felt uncomfortable and inadequate in the moment. 3) Meaning you attached to the experience: I'm not smart like the other kids in the class. I can't learn. The teacher thinks I'm not smart. I'll never be a successful student. The people in my family are all smart, except for me. And so on.

The feelings that arise while these thoughts swirl around are feelings of inadequacy, discomfort, isolation, disconnection, shame, tension, and anxiety, to name a few. These negative emotions surrounding our memory of the event, and can act as the dragon guarding the memory. When we are unwilling to face the dragon of our emotions, we stay stuck in a cycle of repetition. While we are able to see the possibility of a new future, we are unable to move toward it.

By unpacking our stories and separating facts from emotions, and the meaning we have given the experience, we become clear and can speak from the heart. Being able to state what happened without embellishments keeps things clear. That doesn't mean we ignore the feelings that our experiences or those of others evoke in us. Stating how an experience makes us feel is very important and keeps us from blaming others for our feelings. Telling our stories makes us vulnerable, and for people who are already wounded, or fragile, that can be difficult. Telling our stories in a safe and supportive environment can be liberating. When we share our stories the burden lightens.

More often than not, there are two parts to our story: the facts of what happened and the story we build around those facts. The story we build acts like a wall that keeps us safe, but at the same time it keeps us separate. It's important to be conscious of that.

"Listening is an art. Like any art worth mastering, it takes practice." Milagros

Listening and Hearing

Listening is something we do all the time. In fact, we do it so much that sometimes we listen without hearing. There are also times when we hear without listening, as when we happen upon an existing conversation and hear something unintended. When listening and hearing are combined with an open heart and an open mind the experience can be transformative.

Facing the speaker, making eye contact, and having a posture of attention creates a momentary bond between speaker and listener, a bond that, if nurtured, can lead to more, and even deeper, sharing. To listen and to really hear with an open mind and an open heart is to create a supportive space for sharing our stories.

In my "Race Demystified" seminars, I ask participants how they feel after engaging in a listening exercise. More often than not they say, "I felt really heard." Feeling heard keeps us from needing to repeat ourselves. Feeling heard makes us feel cared for and nurtured, and it makes us feel that we are important and that we count.

Listening is paying attention. Listening works best when we can quiet our own inner voices and can allow the voice of the other to penetrate our being and to open our hearts. But most often what we hear is filtered through our life experiences and memories—what we know and believe about a topic, what we have heard or have seen as it relates to a topic. We even bring our lack of information to our experience of listening. And, when it comes to the topic of race, we have many gaps in our knowledge and a great deal of misinformation.

Listening and hearing are choices we make. And how we hear determines how we process the information we receive. We can listen through our anger and pain. We can listen through our connection or our compassion. We can listen through the voices of the past, or the stillness of the present, but, regardless of how we listen, what we hear will determine how we will react.

Deep listening requires that we suspend ourselves, our personality, and what we believe for a moment. It requires that we stop analyzing the speaker or falling into judgment. Deep listening is about creating a quiet space within us that allows the other persons' words to echo back to them. In that echo, they hear their own stories and feel their own pain. Deep listening lets us "feel" the speakers' body language as they express in silence something for which they have no words. In short, deep listening is a practice that can help us to see ourselves in the mirror of the other. As listener we become a comforting agent and a healing balm.

Questioning

How we ask questions and what questions we choose to ask determine the direction a conversation about race will take. Being aware of how we hijack conversations by asking certain questions when we are uncomfortable is key to keeping the conversation moving in the direction of the goal. Awareness of our own discomfort with the topic can help us to become an observer of our reaction.

Resistance to the conversation can show up in a variety of ways, such as checking out mentally or emotionally; giving more attention to the voices in our head than to the voice of the person speaking; asking inappropriate questions aimed at throwing the person of course, or asking questions that are completely off topic.

In my seminars, I engage participants in a particular exercise of listening where they are not allowed to ask questions. While the listener might find it uncomfortable, the speaker who gets to speak without interruption feels really heard.

Still, questions are important for clarification. They can also act as an intervention and can be useful in the process of healing. The right question at the right time can make all the difference in our understanding of the topic at hand.

Before asking questions, take a moment to examine your motivation. Ask questions that are open-ended and that contain within them a desire to know the speaker or the subject better. Be introspective and breathe for a minute with your questions before you ask them.

Processing, in this case is for healing and transformation.

Processing

Most of us are pretty "heady." We need facts and figures to determine if something is worth our time or to judge if it's right or wrong. The problem is that as mentioned before in this book, race is emotional! We can't solve the problems of the heart by simply using our head. We need a combination of both head and heart to make the transformation needed in our racialized nation.

Processing can happen quickly or it can take days, weeks, and even months as the information passes through the filters of our awareness. It is not necessarily about thinking things through. It is more about allowing the information to filter through to the subconscious mind where we might even be given an AHA! We can take information and, trying to make sense of it, mull it around in our heads. But if we really want it to transform us, then it needs that twelve-inch drop into the heart, where we carry our deepest feelings. Only there can it take its proper place. If need be, we might even allow ourselves to be vulnerable enough for the information to break our hearts so that the light of a new awareness can get in and heal us from the inside out.

In our culture, "never let them see you cry" is a motto for many. We want to avoid painful emotions at any cost. But, when it comes to race, emotion is all we are. We feel anger, fear, disconnection, isolation, oppression, guilt, shame and much more. E-motion is moving energy, commonly known as energy in motion. Emotions move us, especially if we are stuck, from where we were to where we could be.

We like things in a nice, neat, predictable package. But emotions are often unpredictable, and, since race is a scary subject to begin with, the thought of adding emotions makes the topic even more frightening. So we are experts at intellectualizing race, while living in denial of its damaging effects. We have more research than we can lay our hands on. We have been counting, measuring, and studying race since the first Africans were brought to the "new world" as free laborers. But all of that science and research means little, if we don't allow our humanity to be touched by the information, and transform us from the inside out.

While books can give us a great deal of information and can speed up the process of healing by giving us some of the missing data, that data still needs to be processed through our emotions. Remember that we cannot solve with our heads an issue that's centered in our heart. Make no mistake about it, race is emotional, and persona! And, when we bravely enter the heart to deal with it, there we encounter the healing crisis.

The crisis happens because where we are now is different from where we are headed, and, in order to get to this new place, we have to shed what we are holding in the present. In other words, we have to release what is familiar, and we resist doing that. As French author André Gide wisely wrote, *"One does not discover new lands without consenting to lose sight of the shore for a very long time."*

THE HEALING CRISIS

"There is no greater chaos than that which happens when we choose to heal." Milagros

The road to healing and transformation is fraught with chaos and upheaval. We choose to engage in a conversation on race, and suddenly our whole world is upside down. In a race conversation people start talking about things that happened hundreds of years ago and that have nothing to do with us today; People say things such as, our family is newly arrived in the country, we had nothing to do with slavery. Or they start talking about things that make us feel unsafe, or like some type of racist.

We often think we know all about race until we engage in conversation and suddenly are faced with a country we didn't know existed and with people we didn't know were having a very different experience from the ones we were having. We saw this happening in New Orleans with Hurricane Katrina:

"Hurricane Katrina exposed the shocking extent to which poverty and income disparities exist in our country," writes The Leadership Conference on Civil and Human Rights. *"For many Americans, the tragedy made visible the unfinished struggle to achieve racial equality and economic justice."*
With that crisis suddenly we were forced to confront a reality we might not have previously known, or were simply in denial of.

While engaging in a conversation on race, some might have found themselves saying, "This certainly is not the country I live in." "I didn't know this history!" Others may have thought, "I don't want to be in this conversation." "Why did I come?" "I need to get out of here. This conversation is making me feel very vulnerable, raw, open, and I have no way of sealing the wound." These are some of the ways that the healing crisis makes us feel, so what's the benefit of going through the crisis?

If we allow ourselves to walk through the discomfort, what we find on the other end is a fully awake and aware human being who will never see the world the same way again. What we encounter is someone with a deeper understanding of what it means to be human and American in today's world and how this land we share is different for everyone. It opens us to the realization that while we will never know everything there is to know about race in America, coming to the conversation with humility and openness can lead to new experiences.

WHEN IT SEEMS ENDLESS

There are times when dealing with race seems endless and hopeless. The problem seems so big that we feel we will drown in it. Don't try to tackle all of it at once; indeed, no one person can. But if each of us picks up the mantle, we can make a vast collective difference. Beginning with self, engaging in self-reflection and inspired dialogue, we can help dismantle the wall of separation by removing our personal "brick." If we each take responsibility for doing that, eventually the wall will crumble.

We can then use the old bricks to build a nation home that is worthy of all of us. We can use our bricks to build a nation in which public safety is about keeping all people safe. We can use the old bricks to build good schools and an educational system that works for all children. We can use the old bricks to build a healthcare system that is truly accessible to all. And we can use our bricks to build organizations that offer a living wage.

It takes considerable energy to maintain a dysfunction. When we liberate ourselves, we find the energy to be creative, to find solutions, and to engage in more empowering endeavors.

Our five-hundred-year-old racial legacy is not relegated to the past, indeed the residue of our racist policies and institutions are still with us. However, when we understand this past, we can make a difference in the present and can impact our collective future.

5. CREATING A VISION

A two-day workshop on race can be intense. A great deal of information is shared with the participants, and they share a good deal of information with each other. They feel a renewed passion and often want to take action to do something that will transform race. But before one can take action, having a vision of the goal can be quite compelling. At the end of every seminar I have the participants create a vision for the future, and it goes something like this:

I tell them to take a slow deep breath and to imagine they are in their late nineties. They have a group of young, multicultural children sitting in front of them who are asking their views on race relations as they existed when they were young versus how they are now that they are in their nineties. I ask participants to share what they tell the children about race.

I go on to set the stage by saying that they've had a long, full life. Race relations are different from how they were when they were young. I tell them to describe what these relationships were like and what they did to contribute to the transformation. What did you do to change the racial climate in America? I ask them, "How did you pull your brick out of the wall of separation? How did you impact change in your families, community, or institutions? What did you do to level the economic field on which those children are playing?" How will you answer their questions? How will you feel at the end of your life? What kind of a world are you leaving them as an inheritance?

One seminar participant, Cheryl Jamison, a lawyer and diversity consultant offered an interesting story about where her imagining ultimately took her:

"In early 2011, I had the pleasure of attending a workshop titled "Race Demystified: A Compassionate, Non-confrontational Approach to Understanding Race in America." As a black female who has grown up in America, I have always been interested in learning how to confront racism in ways that might bring about change.

Workshops such as this one generally provide me with an opportunity to learn some things about myself, and this two-day session was no exception. In the afternoon of the second day, we were asked to get into groups and to imagine we were 90 years old and talking to a group of children about the changes we see in race relations and about how we have contributed to those changes.

The first person talked about some of the changes they 'had seen.' And when it came to answering the question—how they had contributed to those changes—they talked about how they had made changes to their current work. Every person in the group approached the question in the same way, looking at how they could use what they were currently doing to bring about the changes they would like to see in the future. I recall saying that I wanted to hold public dialogues on race. Soon the workshop was over.

The next day, while I was walking to work, the exercise came back to my mind in the form of a more serious question, "So what are you going to do to help bring about the change you would like to see?" A list of things started forming, and one of the items was that I should teach a class on race and conflict at the University of Baltimore. I am a graduate of the University of Baltimore's School of Law, and my current job provided an opportunity for me to be a part of a team that taught a class on conflict resolution in Maryland for the school's Negotiations and Conflict Management program. I also was a guest speaker in several classes taught by my friend, colleague, and co-trainer, Lou Gieszl.

My first thought was that Lou and I could teach a graduate-level class on race and conflict. After some discussion, we decided I would teach the class and he would be a guest speaker. The idea was presented to the Program Director, and in January 2012 I began teaching a "Race and Conflict" seminar to 17 undergraduate majors in the Government and Public Policy program. It was not exactly the audience I had in mind, but I was grateful for the opportunity. The class was a big success though. Students learned a bit of history and they learned about their own biases as well as how to have a conversation about race. Two weeks before the end of the semester, I was asked to teach "Race and Conflict" as a graduate summer course.

This all came about because of a question posed at the end of the two-day workshop "Race Demystified: A Compassionate, Non-confrontational Approach to Understanding Race in

America." Thanks for moving me from thinking to doing. Thanks for changing my life."

Not everyone may feel as inspired as Cheryl did after she took the workshop, but every person can contribute in one way or another to dismantle our collective dysfunction, which we call race.

6. COMMITTING TO WHOLENESS

Many years ago, while I was studying to be a Reiki master and teacher, the first thing I learned was that healing is a do-it-yourself process. The best that anyone other than oneself can do is to facilitate that process. The second thing I learned is that what we commit to we experience. There is a vast difference between a commitment to healing and a commitment to wholeness.

Wholeness is being all of what we are at any given moment in time with the possibility of all that we can be. It is about the totality of what we are in the constant evolutionary state we call life. It is about allowing all that we are in the present, a composite of our past with an eye towards the future. Once we understand healing and begin that process, we need to set our vision on wholeness.

When it comes to race, wholeness means that we leave behind the racialized self. It also means creating a new identity, one founded on the reality of one human family sharing the land and resources on the planet with seven billion others, some whom we love and some whom we fear. Wholeness is the awareness that everything impacts our lives and that we all are connected through a vast, unbroken, invisible biological chain, and the web we call life.

7. TAKING ACTION

Conversations are just the beginning. We need to pull our energy and our resources together to take action—and, dare I say, to take *inspired* action—so that we can enact change. At the end of all my seminars, after I have participants work together to create a vision of what our nation looks like without the burden of division based on race, I ask them to commit to something they believe they can do to make things better. What they commit to ranges from continuing to learn about the nation's history to becoming more self-reflective to simply giving the matter more thought. Or one could be as inspired as Cheryl.

One thoughtful participant said this about her commitment: "*After doing a nine-week program on healing from racism, I realized that the only way I could use white privilege in a positive way was to* speak out against it. I learned that I had to work to educate white people about systemic racism; otherwise, I was leaving non-white people to do it, which is not fair. Now I think more about how my words and actions can either contribute to racism or can help to dismantle it. I think the only way to counter racism or to make race a part of the conversation in my field (healthcare) or in society in general is to educate people about the effects of racism on all of us and to make it safe to discuss the topic. We have to take the defensiveness and blame out of the equation and acknowledge how racism harms us all in different ways: it causes discrimination against people of color and fragility and infantilism in white people. Then and only then can we talk about how to move forward and create a better and more just society for everyone."

Everyone can do something right where they are. Everyone has the power to bring about change and to impact the lives of those around them compassionately. So, what will you say you did to turn the tide of racism in our nation? What legacy will you leave the children?

8.BECOMING A LIVING BRIDGE

Each one of us has a wonderful opportunity to become a living bridge to peace and well-being. Our conversations on race are vital to beginning that process. A bridge is a connector. It stands in troubled water with unwavering strength, conviction, and stillness. It is made of pillars that hold up the path on which others will cross and stands the test of time.

Moreover, a bridge stands between the shadow and the light, facing day and night with the same conviction—to see that all who need to cross are able to do so. And, it allows us to explore new lands and new opportunities by being the connecting structure that spans the gap.

As a living bridge we facilitate the passing of one experience to another. We create opportunities for people to come together for conversation and sharing. We hold a vision of wholeness for ourselves that allows for others to be authentic with us, and we allow ourselves and others the freedom to feel our feelings and our emotions. We believe in people's ability to change, and we trust those changes will take place in their own divine timeframe. While we may want others to come to the table to speak about race NOW, we know they will do so when they are ready. But this does not keep us from offering them the opportunity to become literate about race.

CONCLUSION
CONSIDER RACE

Things have been so unbalanced for so long that, in order to bring them back to center, we must consider race as part of every decision we make as a nation. As mentioned before in this book, when making policies or laws, we must consider the impact they will have on people at the lowest socioeconomic levels, which most often means people of color. Before writing another history book, we must consider the impact of telling yet another Eurocentric tale and what that tale would be like if told by people of color. Consider who is at the table when policies are made and laws are being written that affect people we know only by reading about them in a book, or some statistic on a research project.

Human beings are creatures of community, so, when it comes to creating, we create for that which is around us, for that which benefits us, and for those with whom we are involved. This doesn't make us bad people; it simply makes us human.

But human beings are also creatures of imagination with the capacity to step into someone else's shoes. We have the power of vision, which can expand our reach to other universes. Consider the nation we could become if we lead with race, at least till we bring our country into balance. if we make race a leading part of every important conversation and decision, with the goal of reaching equity. If we took every component of our society and measured every institution by how it's serving ALL Americans, and, as a result, we began to adjust, change, and transform, what would happen? Who might we become as people, as a nation? What legacy would we leave our children?

We are extraordinary creatures, capable of great feats! We have the power of love on our side. Love in action is unstoppable! I challenge all of us to put it to practice around this thing we invented called race and to see what happens. Cheryl's project is a great example of love in action.

In Conclusion, everyone can do something to make a difference. Together we are unstoppable!

REFERENCES

"Civil Rights Implications of Rebuilding the Gulf."
The Leadership Conference: Poverty & Hurricane
Katrina.
http://www.civilrights.org/poverty/katrina/?referre
r=https://search.yahoo.com/
Gide, André. Quote.
http://www.brainyquote.com/quotes/authors/a/an
dre_gide.html
Holder, Eric. Department of Justice African-
American History Month Program. February 18,
2009.
https://www.justice.gov/opa/speech/attorney-
general-eric-holder-department-justice-african-
american-history-month-program
Linshi, Jack. "Starbucks Baristas Will Stop Writing
'Race Together' on Your Cups," Time, March 22,
2015. http://time.com/3753493/starbucks-race-
together-barista/
"On Views of Race and Inequality, Blacks and
Whites Are Worlds Apart." Pew   Research
Center: Social & Demographic Trends, June 21,
2016.
http://www.pewsocialtrends.org/2016/06/27/on-
views-of-race-and-   inequality-blacks-and-whites-
are-worlds-apart/st_2016-06-27_race-
        inequality-overview-01/

"Reproductive Health: Infant Mortality." CDC Centers for Disease Control and Prevention. http://www.cdc.gov/reproductivehealth/MaternalInfantHealth/InfantMortality.htm

"When the Bough Breaks," *Unnatural Causes: Is Inequality Making Us Sick*, Episode 2. California News Reel. http://newsreel.org/video/UNNATURAL-CAUSES

"List of Country by Infant Mortality Rate," The World Health Organization (WHO), 2015, Wikipedia: https://en.wikipedia.org/wiki/List_of_countries_by_infant_mortality_rate

"The Night Tulsa Burned," In Search of History, TV Movie February, 1999. https://www.youtube.com/watch?v=LD3aw4-RJpE

ABOUT THE AUTHOR

Milagros Phillips is also the author of 11 REASONS TO BECOME RACE LITERATE: A Pocket Guide to a New Conversation. She has spent the last 25 years bringing race literacy to colleges, universities, national leaders, corporations, and non-profits with her historically grounded, race-based seminars and programs. A speaker, an artist, and a freelance consultant, she may be reached at: info@milagrosphillips.com

Made in the USA
Coppell, TX
10 June 2020